She Believed She Could So She Did

A MODERN WOMAN'S GUIDE TO LIFE

SAM LACEY

summersdale

SHE BELIEVED SHE COULD SO SHE DID

An Hachette UK Company
www.hachette.co.uk

Summersdale Publishers Ltd
Part of Octopus Publishing Group Limited
Carmelite House
50 Victoria Embankment
LONDON
EC4Y 0DZ
UK

www.summersdale.com

Printed and bound in China

ISBN: 978-1-78783-561-0

Contents

Introduction

Well done for picking up *She Believed She Could So She Did* – you won't regret it. Its pages are filled with fabulous tips, helpful advice and plenty of inspiration to help you live your best life and achieve your dreams, whether that's doing more of what you love, getting fit, finding happiness in your workplace, overcoming fears and personal challenges, or simply being at peace with yourself. Every woman is unique, with a wealth of different strengths and, whether together or alone, when we put our minds to it we can achieve remarkable things. Whatever you aspire to do, this little book will be right there with you.

PART ONE:
Who Run the World?

To inspire and encourage you in your own endeavours, this section takes a look at some amazing ladies – past and present – who have absolutely rocked it; in some cases they actually changed the course of history. From sporting legends and lady racers to scientists and conservationists, they have forged the way with their perseverance, determination, ideas and independence. Remember: we are all extraordinary in our own way. Take a leaf from the book of some of these game-changers and you'll be onto a winner!

You have the power

Never doubt that you have the power within you to instigate huge change. Climate activist Greta Thunberg is demonstrating to us all what can be achieved when we are brimming with determination, passion and belief. She has sparked a revolution, showing that others will stop, listen and pay attention when they are truly inspired by someone's cause.

**DON'T THINK ABOUT MAKING WOMEN
FIT THE WORLD — THINK ABOUT
MAKING THE WORLD FIT WOMEN.**

Gloria Steinem

You are capable, you are strong

Women inspire women. In 1973, 29-year-old US tennis player Billie Jean King – the world's number one female player – competed in a match against former Wimbledon men's champion Bobby Riggs, bringing gender equality into the mainstream. The match was watched on TV by an estimated 90 million people worldwide. A few years before the game-changing match, she had also formed an independent women-only tour with eight other female players, in protest at having lower pay than their male counterparts. With her victory over Bobby Riggs, this determined lady continued to shape the future of women in sport.

One giant step... for women

Everyone knows who first set foot on the moon, but little is known of the women who helped to make these missions happen. In 1962, NASA mathematician Katherine Johnson worked on the detailed calculations and equations needed to successfully complete astronaut John Glenn's journey into orbit. She also played a pivotal behind-the-scenes role in the 1969 moon landings themselves.

DON'T BE AFRAID TO BE A LIONESS IN A LION'S WORLD;

YOUR ROAR IS JUST AS LOUD

WOMEN SPEAKING UP FOR THEMSELVES AND FOR THOSE AROUND THEM IS THE STRONGEST FORCE WE HAVE TO CHANGE THE WORLD.

Melinda Gates

Breaking new ground

If there was ever a role-model for twenty-first-century girl power, it's singer and songwriter Taylor Swift. By the age of 16 she was already an award-winning country music artist and over the last several years she has transformed herself into an undeniable queen of the charts. We're not saying everyone has to become a musical sensation, but her drive and determination to succeed as a woman in a man's world can definitely be taken as inspiration.

Live your life
in the fast lane

Born in 1882, young Dorothy Levitt went from working as a secretary at the Napier motor company to becoming the first British woman racing driver. She even gave driving lessons to royalty! To dispense with the belief that women weren't strong enough to be behind the wheel, she also wrote articles for the general and motoring press maintaining that it was possible to be both feminine and capable of controlling a racing car. In 1909 Dorothy published a book, called *The Woman and the Car*. Among the book's many helpful pieces of advice was a tip about carrying a small hand mirror. As well as being able to check your appearance when you arrived at your destination, it could also double as a rear-view mirror – an idea that manufacturers began to introduce in 1914. This fashionable queen of speed was an inspiration for generations of capable female drivers worldwide.

THE SKY
IS FULL
OF STARS;
MAKE YOURS
SHINE THE
BRIGHTEST

Aim high!

Japanese mountaineer Junko Tabei was the first woman to reach the summit of Mount Everest – a feat she achieved in 1975 at just 35 years old. Her journey started at university, where she wished to join an all-male alpine club. After graduation, Junko formed the first ladies' climbing club in Japan and, after scaling Mount Fuji and then the Matterhorn in the Alps, she led a team of female mountaineers to the top of the highest mountain in the world, surviving an avalanche on the way. If anyone ever doubted that women could climb mountains, Tabei proved them wrong once and for all.

There's something so special about a woman who dominates in a man's world.

Rihanna

Speak out without fear

Remember that you can always beat the odds. When she was 15, Malala Yousafzai survived being shot by terrorists as she travelled home on a bus. She had been targeted for being outspoken about women and children's rights to education in Pakistan. After recovering, she went on to become a prominent activist for education and human rights, and she co-founded the Malala Fund, a charity that fights for girls' education. Malala was also awarded the Nobel Peace Prize at just 17 years old.

Shoot for the stars

Women have been pushing the boundaries of their knowledge for many years. In the eighteenth century, German-born Caroline Herschel was way ahead of her time, working to become the first professional female astronomer. She executed many of the calculations for her brother William's work and, in 1786, she was the first woman to spot a comet; the first of eight that she would find over the following 11 years.

Trust in yourself

Along with her research colleagues, Jane Goodall and Dian Fossey, conservationist and primatologist Biruté Galdikas broke down academic barriers in the 1960s and 1970s with her study of orangutans. She was told that it would be impossible to locate these elusive primates as they lived so remotely, but she believed differently. After obtaining funding for her study, she left the US in 1971, headed to the jungles of Borneo and was successful. Having located the orangutans, she established Camp Leakey – which still functions as a base for research scientists today – and, in 1986, she set up Orangutan Foundation International, a non-profit organization dedicated to the conservation of wild orangutans. In 1997 she was the first non-Indonesian woman to be awarded the country's "Hero for the Earth" award. Her dedication and passion serve as an example to us all about what can be achieved with hard work and perseverance.

Dust off your tiara and show them who rules

Be a leader

Oprah Winfrey is undoubtedly one of the
most influential women in America today.
As well as a talk show host and actor, she
is also well known as a philanthropist and
advocate of racial and gender equality. In 2007
she founded the Oprah Winfrey Leadership
Academy for Girls in South Africa; a project
she developed and funded. Then, in 2018 she
became the first African American woman
to receive the Cecil B. DeMille Award at the
Golden Globes for lifetime achievement.
Now there's a woman to be inspired by!

WE VERY MUCH
UNDERSTAND
THAT IT TAKES
BOLD
VOICES AND
BOLD
STEPS TO MAKE
THINGS CHANGE.

Megan Rapinoe

Leave the
haters where they belong:

in your rear-view
mirror

Embrace your inner icon

You need only walk into any department store to see (or smell!) French fashion legend Coco Chanel's lasting legacy. As well as a designer, Coco was an excellent businesswoman. Her beginnings were spent in relative poverty, and she learned to sew when she was growing up in an orphanage. Finding a financial backer allowed her to open a boutique in 1913, which became popular with well-off ladies. As her empire expanded, she launched her first fragrance – the world-famous Chanel No. 5 – in the 1920s. Appealing to the independent women of her time, Coco Chanel also introduced the "little black dress", which, along with her other timeless and elegant designs, is still the staple of many a wardrobe today. Not only did her business become a financial success, but Coco broke the glass ceiling of her era to become one of the most iconic women in the world. Today, a bottle of Chanel No. 5 is sold somewhere in the world every 30 seconds. If that's not a lasting legacy, we don't know what is!

Women wear the trousers

Katharine Hepburn was a Hollywood force of nature. She starred in a plethora of movies and TV programmes from the 1930s through to the 1990s. Off-screen she was renowned for her fierce independence and lively personality; she often went make-up-free, and she broke the mould by wearing trousers before it became widely acceptable for women to do so, leading to many others following her example. She led an active lifestyle, swimming daily and even playing tennis into her eighties.

Figuring out that
I'm not going to
figure it out has
been the biggest
and most liberating
revelation of my life.

Jameela Jamil

If the slipper fits,
give it back to
Prince Charming;
you've got this

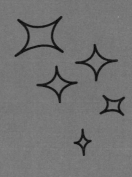

Write your own destiny

Who hasn't heard of J. K. Rowling? From humble beginnings (she wrote her first book while raising her daughter as a single parent), she has become one of the most recognized women in the world. The first Harry Potter book was reportedly turned down by 12 publishers before being signed up, but the series has now sold over 500 million copies worldwide. As well as writing, she has founded a not-for-profit organization that works to end the institutionalization of children around the world. Simply magic.

Branch out on your own

Never be afraid to go it alone – just like Valentina Tereshkova. The Russian engineer and cosmonaut was the very first woman to travel alone into space and to this day she remains the only female to have carried out a solo space mission. Her *Vostok 6* spacecraft took off in June 1963, and orbited Earth 48 times over three days. Unlike other astronauts, Valentina had not had any formal pilot training, but was a well-practised amateur parachutist; these skills were useful as, at the time, cosmonauts had to parachute from their capsule before it hit the ground when they returned to Earth. After her space adventure, she embarked on a political career and twice received the Order of Lenin, an award bestowed for outstanding achievements in research, art, economics or technology.

WELL-BEHAVED WOMEN SELDOM MAKE HISTORY.

Laurel Thatcher Ulrich

Step outside the box

New Zealand Prime Minister Jacinda Ardern is the youngest leader the country has had; she took up the post at just 37 years old. She is widely acknowledged and praised for her characteristics of inclusion, compassion, empathy and understanding. She has had a baby while in office, famously attending the UN General Assembly with her three-month-old daughter. She also welcomed government reforms for families in a video filmed from her sofa while she was on maternity leave. Now that's multitasking.

Smart women speak their minds

Setting a modest example

Providing a role model in sport for Muslim women and girls across the globe is Ibtihaj Muhammad. She was the first woman to wear a hijab in the Olympics, while competing as part of the 2016 US sabre-fencing team. She finished in bronze position; also the first time a Muslim-American female athlete had won an Olympic medal. Since her sporting success, Ibtihaj has founded her own modest-clothing line.

I want to encourage women to embrace their own uniqueness.

Miranda Kerr

Know your own brilliant mind

Where would we all be without Wi-Fi? Did you know it was a woman who helped to invent the technology that we use for today's wireless communications? Hedy Lamarr was born in Vienna in 1914 and entered the Hollywood spotlight in the 1930s. Although she was a successful actor, it was her passion for science experiments, and meeting writer George Antheil at a dinner party in 1940, that led to her second career. George shared Hedy's interest in inventing, and, with a war looming, they worked together to develop a "frequency hopping" communication system, intended for use in guiding torpedoes. Although it wasn't actually used by the military, her invention went on to be the foundation for "spread spectrum" communication technology, which is the very thing that today's Bluetooth and Wi-Fi utilize. In her later life, Hedy's technology was recognized and rewarded when she became the first woman to receive the Invention Convention's BULBIE Gnass Spirit of Achievement Award. In 2014 she was also inducted into the National Inventors Hall of Fame.

WAKE UP AND BE FABULOUS!

Be a role model

Body activist Ashley Graham made history and changed the public's perception of what a model should look like when she became the first ever plus-sized model (the fashion industry's term, rather than hers!) to appear on the cover of *Sports Illustrated* in 2016. As well as a successful modelling career, she has given a number of talks on body positivity and self-acceptance, becoming an inspiring role model for women around the world.

FIND OUT WHO YOU ARE
AND BE THAT PERSON.

Ellen DeGeneres

PART TWO:
Be Your Own Woman

Independence is life-affirming! It can be tempting to benchmark ourselves against other people; we look at what they're doing... how many activities they seem to be juggling... and wonder why we're not measuring up. But this is your life and you should be doing what YOU want to do. What are your life goals? What do you want to achieve? What brings you joy? Are you doing enough of it and, if not, how can you make more time? This section contains tips on how to liberate yourself and shape a life that you are satisfied with. Serenity and contentment are within your grasp!

Fall in love with yourself

One of the first steps on the path to independence is to become confident in your own skin. Are you completely happy with the person in the mirror? If not, then do something about that. Make an "all about me" list. What do you see as your strengths? What do other people like about you? Which are your best bits? Add to your list every time someone pays you a compliment or you do something you're proud of. Keep it to hand and refer to it when self-doubt pops up.

Once upon
a time, there
was a girl who
did exactly as
she pleased

Learn to say "no, thank you"

Saying "no, thank you" to things you don't want to do will leave you more time to say "yes, please" to those you do. But why do we find saying "no" so difficult? It could be we're worried about letting someone down – especially if it's someone we are close to or keen to impress. It could also be that you're concerned about what others will think of you. And it's really tricky to turn someone's invitation down in person. However, it can be worse to agree to something and then back out as the event draws closer, or to go along and then spend the whole time wishing you were somewhere else. If you want to turn someone down but don't want to appear rude, simply ask if you can think about it, which will give you some time to come up with an excuse. Even better, be honest and explain that you don't want to go; although being comfortable doing this might need practice!

You're only human.
You live once and life
is wonderful, so eat the
damned red velvet cupcake.

Emma Stone

YOU
are your
number
ONE
priority

Rest up!

You can't spend time doing the things you love if you don't have the energy to do them, so take care of your body and mind. Make sure you get enough sleep – as well as resting your limbs, sleep allows your brain to process the information from the day – drink plenty of water and enjoy treats in moderation. As long as you don't overdo it, it's OK to eat that Friday doughnut!

I'M JUST TRYING TO CHANGE THE WORLD ONE SEQUIN AT A TIME.

Lady Gaga

Get a step ahead

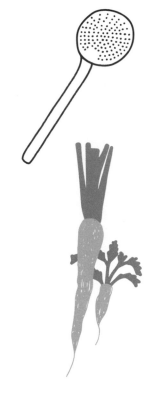

One of the easiest ways to make better use of your time is to plan out your meals for the week and buy what you need in one go. If you're a "drop into the shops on the way home" kind of gal, then try changing your habits – even for a short time – and see how it feels. Make a list of your dinners for the week, buy your ingredients and then stick the list of your meals on the fridge. Day to day you'll have one less thing to think about, freeing up brain space to think about other stuff. If you're feeling really adventurous, why not treat yourself to a slow cooker so you can throw your ingredients in the pot on your way out in the morning and come home to a healthy home-cooked feast? There are lots of recipe ideas online – and making double quantities and freezing some means you're ahead of the game the following week too. Just think how much extra time you could create for yourself then!

Recipe

_____

_____

_____

_____

_____

_____

_____

_____

_____

_____

_____

_____

_____

_____

THE ONLY PERMISSION YOU NEED IS YOUR OWN

Trust your own judgement

Part of being self-sufficient is learning to make your own choices and stick by them. If you have a decision to make, no matter how large or small, compile a list of pros and cons. Remember that sometimes you might need to take a risk to achieve maximum reward. And it's still OK to ask other people for advice; being independent doesn't mean being insular.

LIVING OUT LOUD IS LIVING A LIFE THAT'S BIGGER THAN YOURSELF...

YOU LEAVE SOMETHING ON THIS EARTH THAT'S BIGGER THAN YOURSELF.

Viola Davis

Spend less time online

How many hours do you spend online, surfing entertainment websites, window shopping and scrolling through social media? Recent research has shown we spend an average of 3 hours and 15 minutes on our phones every day, with the top 20 per cent of us busting the 4-hour mark! On the surface, this may not sound like much – but this actually equates to 1,186 hours, or 49.5 days, a year. Just imagine how all of that time each day could be put to better use: calling up a loved one for a chat, spending time with friends, exercising or taking up a new hobby, having a clear-out of items you could donate to charity, sleeping, the list goes on... Try downloading an app like Mute, which tracks your screen time and challenges you to break your digital habits. Or you could decide to have one or two completely phone-free days each week – now there's a personal challenge.

Expand your hobby horizons

Learning new things keeps our brains active, so if you don't already have a hobby then why not take one up? From simple activities like reading, sudoku and jigsaws, to boxing, singing and abseiling, there are many things you could get up to in your spare time. Setting aside even a little time in the day to do something just for yourself will relax and recharge you. Who cares if your office colleagues hit the shops while you go off to the staffroom and knit? If you enjoy it, do it!

Destination: Diva!

Always be
a first-rate
version of
yourself,
instead of a
second-rate
version of
someone else.

Judy Garland

Put the "me" into "we"

If you're in a relationship, of course it's lovely to do things together – but you don't need to be joined at the hip 100 per cent of the time. It's really important to take some time for yourself, so perhaps you could make one night a week just for you, or have a regular standing date with friends rather than your partner. Your other half may not share your passion for pottery painting – and that's OK!

Going solo

Don't be afraid to venture out on your own. If the thought of sitting in a restaurant alone bothers you, then hit a coffee shop instead and take a book, or just people-watch. You could even indulge in a spa weekend on your own; it's more relaxing when you don't have to make conversation. And if nobody is free and there's a movie you really want to see, go to see it on your own – plus, you'll get the whole extra-large carton of popcorn to yourself. Bonus.

Do what you want, when you want, how you want

Dress to impress (yourself)

Many of us feel pressure to wear particular kinds of clothes, whether it comes from society – dressing in a certain way for our gender – or more generally by colleagues, family and friends. But that doesn't have to be the case, because you're in control. Of course, there are certain situations when it might be prudent to dress smartly – an interview, for example – and in some workplaces, a professional appearance is expected. But how you dress should make you feel good about yourself and empower you, and it *is* possible to be both presentable and comfortable at the same time. If you need some help with your style, try a shop with a free personal shopper service. And if you choose to throw on your fluffy penguin pyjamas as soon as you're home, no one has to know...

Your self-worth is determined by you. You don't have to depend on someone telling you who you are.

Beyoncé

YOU DON'T NEED A CAPE AND TIGHTS TO BE A SUPERHERO

DON'T WASTE YOUR ENERGY TRYING TO CHANGE OPINIONS. DO YOUR THING, AND DON'T CARE IF THEY LIKE IT.

Tina Fey

Organize your time to suit you

Are you an early bird or a night owl? Some of us function better in the morning, and others prefer to burn the midnight oil. Try adjusting your daily routine to make best use of the time when you're most productive. Whether you get up half an hour earlier to plan for the day ahead, or opt for a late-evening gym session before you go to bed, do what works for your rhythm.

Search for your sunshine among the clouds

TO ME, GETTING ON THE
WORST-DRESSED LIST
IS JUST AS GOOD AS GETTING
ON THE BEST-DRESSED LIST.

Rose Byrne

Choose your company wisely

The people you spend time with should understand that you sometimes need to do your own thing. If they don't, perhaps you should look for new people to hang out with! Don't depend on others to make you happy; you can do that yourself. Friends should support and encourage, not expect you to go along with the crowd. Learning to recognize that some people's influence can be unhealthy might be tricky – and you might need to summon some courage to disconnect from them; but in the long run you'll be the one who benefits.

Look after the pennies

Getting a grip on your spending is a
first-class way to feel in control of your
life. If you're wasting cash on stuff you
don't need and forever fire-fighting your
bank account, you won't have the funds
available to buy the more important things
that you really want. Why not use one of
the many apps now available to keep track
of your monthly incomings and outgoings?
If you're tempted to use your credit card
when you go shopping, leave it at home
and take cash instead, and if you're
shopping online let things sit in your
basket for a while before you check out
to make sure you really can't do without
them. It's also wise to save some money
for a rainy day; life doesn't always pan
out the way we think it will and having a
financial cushion can absorb the impact
of any curveballs that might come your
way. Independent women plan ahead!

Count your blessings

A brilliant way to assert your independence is to take stock. Take a look at what's great in your life right now – this can be absolutely anything, as long as it's personal to you. Think big (good health, family and friends) or small (your new shoes didn't rub your feet!). Make a list at the end of each day of all the things you are thankful for and use these for inspiration as you move on through your life. Enjoy the moment!

My mother told me to be a lady. And for her, that meant be your own person, be independent.

Ruth Bader Ginsburg

PART THREE:
Achieve and Succeed

Want some help figuring out whether you're in the right job? Wondering how to get the career you desire? Looking for some inspiration for how you can enrich your life through helping others? Then this section is just what you need. It'll provide you with some ideas and tips for all of this, as well as some advice on how to keep yourself motivated, stand out from the crowd and smash through any obstacles in the path to your dreams. So read on to learn how to stop holding yourself back. Grow wings and aim high!

Take stock

Most of us will spend a third of our lives at work, so shouldn't it be spent doing something we want to do? Not every day is going to be perfect – we all have days when we find it hard to summon the enthusiasm to leave the duvet – but if you spend the majority of your workdays wishing that you were somewhere else, then perhaps it's time for a rethink. If you've been in the same place for a while, it might be daunting to think about moving on. But you know yourself the best; if it's not right, follow your heart and take a leap of faith.

BE THE MASTER OF YOUR MOJO!

How we spend
our days is,
of course,
how we spend
our lives.

Annie Dillard

Little Miss Motivator

Even if your current job isn't ideal, it's still possible to keep motivated and think about your longer-term goals at the same time. Look for the positives in your day-to-day interactions – do you have a laugh with your colleagues? Often the people you spend time with will make a boring day much more bearable. Could you mentor someone, or are there outside-of-work social events that you could attend? Getting to know your work associates better can often lead to new friendships, which in turn will make it easier to look forward to a day at the office. At the same time, think about what your ultimate career goals are. Do you want to stay in the same place and look for a different position, or do you crave a complete change of direction? Writing down your personal goals or making a list of the things you love can often prompt ideas for a dream role. If you decide you need to retrain, there are plenty of eLearning and distance-learning opportunities available. Or you could go old-school and check out a local evening class.

HOW CAN YOU
EXPECT ANYONE
TO BELIEVE IN
YOU AND YOUR
IDEAS IF YOU
DON'T BELIEVE IN
THEM YOURSELF?

Kelly Hoppen

KICK THAT COMFORT ZONE TO THE KERB

Socialize in style

If you want to progress in your current career, do remember to act professionally if you're out socially with your colleagues. To keep your wits about you, try making every other drink non-alcoholic, or choose to stick to the soft stuff – and always make sure you eat something, too. Remember: dancing on the table in front of your boss is unlikely to get you a promotion!

An important
attribute of success
is to be yourself.
Never hide what
makes you, you.

Indra Nooyi

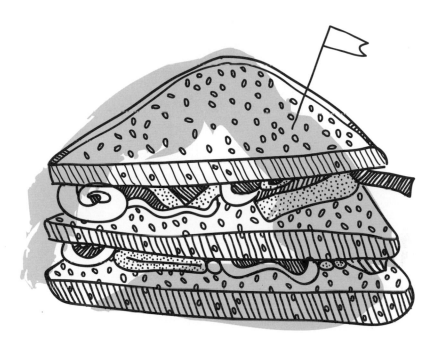

Look at me!

One way to attract attention in the right way at your workplace is by going the extra mile for your colleagues. Can you spare some time to help somebody struggling with their workload? Could you grab a sandwich for someone who forgot their lunch? Kindness costs nothing and, as well as making you feel good, it'll also raise your head above the crowd.

Turn your passion into cash

Another excellent way to redirect your career is to turn a hobby that you love into an extra earner. You may have to start small, doing this on the side while you work, but nowadays there are plenty of ways to do this. If you're creative and crafty, online marketplaces such as eBay and Etsy mean that you can set up shop and make things to order in your free time. To build brand awareness, there may be a local market in your area where you can go along and sell to customers face-to-face. If you're the person who always spots grammar mistakes, could you do proofreading in the evenings? If you're a natural teacher, could you tutor one or two evenings a week? As your side-hustle expands, over time it could have the potential to become your main income. (Do bear in mind that any side income could have tax implications so always check with an accountant or your tax office.)

Speak up

Job satisfaction isn't all about the money – but let's be honest, it does help. If you feel as though you're being overlooked financially, raise it with the appropriate person. You can do it tactfully without shouting your demands; and remember, nobody ever lost out by asking. You should expect to be rewarded what you're worth; if you're not, then move on!

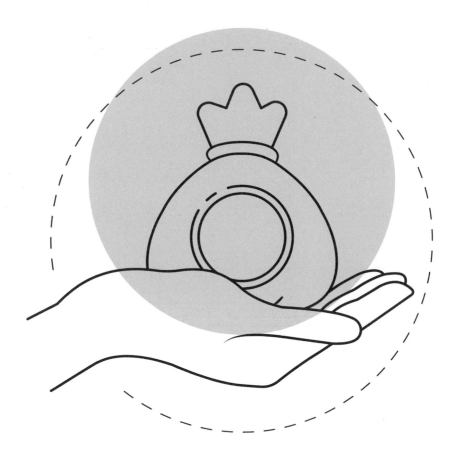

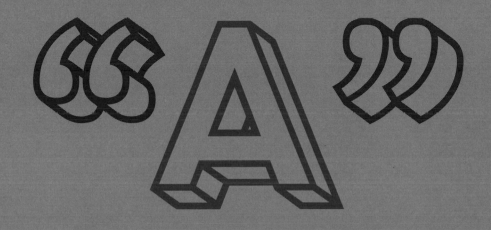

IS FOR

ATTITUDE!

IF YOU DON'T LIKE THE ROAD YOU'RE
WALKING, START PAVING ANOTHER ONE.

Dolly Parton

Care about a cause

Empower yourself by helping others. If you have a cause that you care about, pitch in and help out. Search online for opportunities: supporting a food bank or a homeless shelter, or getting involved with Scouting, are just a few ideas to get you started. Not only is it a brilliant way to contribute to your local or an overseas community and make new acquaintances, but it will give you a huge confidence boost and strengthen your CV too.

Seek out a role model

If you have a particular goal or career in mind, one of the best ways of achieving it is to find a role model. The idea is not to compare yourself to them, but rather to use them as inspiration. Make a mood board with notes to yourself and tips and quotes from this person. It doesn't necessarily have to be someone famous; it could be a former colleague, or someone who you used to go to school or university with.

inspire

What are their skills and attributes? What path have they taken to get to where they are? Have they done any formal training? If you're not directly in touch with a particular person you'd like to emulate, find them on LinkedIn or Facebook and drop them an email to say hi. Having a role model means being able to use other people's knowledge and expertise to drive your enthusiasm and send you along your own path to success.

You are the captain
of your own ship;
steer it in whichever
direction you choose

Sell yourself (part one)

Of course we're talking metaphorically! If you've decided a career move is right for you, make sure your résumé is up-to-date and if you don't have a LinkedIn profile, set one up; 90 per cent of recruiters now use LinkedIn to search for candidates. Don't forget to list any volunteering that you've done or do regularly; many employers will look favourably on this, especially if it's in a complementary area. Be proud of how incredible you are and show off without shame!

Women are the largest untapped reservoir of talent in the world.

Hillary Clinton

Sell yourself (part two)

So the day has arrived: your "dream job" interview. First, tell yourself that you can do this. Write notes about the key points you want to get across and don't forget to prepare some questions for your interviewer; this shows that you are interested in them and the role too. If you're having an online interview, it's just as important to dress appropriately as it is for an interview in person. Remember to check your webcam view beforehand, and move anything unsuitable out of view. You probably don't want your potential employer to see your underwear drying on the radiator behind you!

REBEL LADIES REAP THEIR REWARDS

Try something new

Keeping yourself active and healthy is vital for your well-being, and challenging yourself to try something new on a daily, weekly, monthly or annual basis is a marvellous way to achieve this. Don't save new activities for new year's resolutions – research has shown that 92 per cent of us don't stick to these – so do them now! What is it that fires you up? Do you want to do something physical, mental or both? Taking up a sport, for example, can be invigorating and as well as improving your fitness, it alleviates stress and clears your head. Investigate the groups local to you and enjoy the support of other people as you run, swim or play. Or you could simply decide to eat an extra piece of fruit every day or download an app and learn a language on your lunch break. Take up baking or skateboarding, or leap out of a plane for charity – the choices are endless. Whatever you do, do it for you.

DELETE THE NEGATIVE; ACCENTUATE THE POSITIVE.

Donna Karan

Mind over matter

No matter how much we want to do something new, one of the biggest obstacles we often face is ourselves. We have a habit of getting in our own way, whether it's because of doubts, fears or negative past experiences. However, the very fact that you encounter this kind of roadblock means that you're moving forward toward your goal. Practise saying "I have strength; I can do this" when you feel self-doubt creeping in and don't give up. Believe in yourself, babe!

Embrace the fear

Another barrier to success in life is simply being afraid to try new things in the first place. But awareness of fear is one of the things that defines us; it can make us feel alive. It's perfectly natural to be afraid to try new things, but the only person holding you back is you. If you wait to feel safe before you try new things, you may not ever leave your comfort zone. Woman up. Power on.

Today's
mistakes are
tomorrow's
learning
opportunities!

i'd rather regret
the risk that
didn't work out
than the chances i
didn't take at all.

Simone Biles

Remember why you're here

Career and professional aspirations are of course worthwhile, but remember to balance these with your personal goals and challenges. Live in the moment, value your friendships and your family and draw upon them daily for inspiration and advice. Keep your dreams in the forefront of your mind and the sky's the limit.

SASSY LADIES SAY "I CAN"

PART FOUR:
Give a Little Respect

Who loves ya, baby? You do! The most important person in your life should be you. Learning to adore yourself should be top of any to-do list; if you like and respect who you see in the mirror, then others will follow your example. Value what you do, talk yourself up and boost your self-esteem with the helpful advice in this final part of the book. Read about ways to calm yourself, including mindfulness and meditation; discover the power of positive thinking; find out how a healthy body equals a healthy mind; and uncover why you shouldn't ever compare yourself to others people's "perfect" lifestyles.

Nobody's perfect

One thing to always remember is that the lifestyle your friends display on social media isn't representative of everyday life; it's usually just a snapshot of what they want other people to see. They may not show it, but they're still taking out the bins and cleaning the toilet! It can be incredibly demotivating, not to mention a knock to your self-esteem, to compare yourself to other people's picture-perfect "online story" and wonder why your kitchen doesn't sparkle or why you don't look immaculate when you wake up (hint: neither do they). Remember that it's curated, and only the highlight reel of someone's life, because, behind the scenes, they will have as many ups and downs as the rest of us. If you find yourself feeling deflated by others' boasting, simply scroll on past and concentrate on all the wonderful parts of your own reality.

i WANT TO BE THE PERSON WHO **FEELS GREAT IN HER BODY** AND CAN SAY THAT SHE LOVES iT AND DOESN'T WANT TO CHANGE ANYTHING.

Emma Watson

What is self-esteem, anyway?

Self-esteem is, in essence, how much you value and
like yourself. You can also think of it in terms of self-
worth. It's an important personal trait, as it affects
the decisions you make and how you approach
opportunities in life. Low self-esteem can stop you from
trying new things and make you shy away from the
limelight. This is not what we want for you! You need
to exit your comfort zone to achieve your dreams.

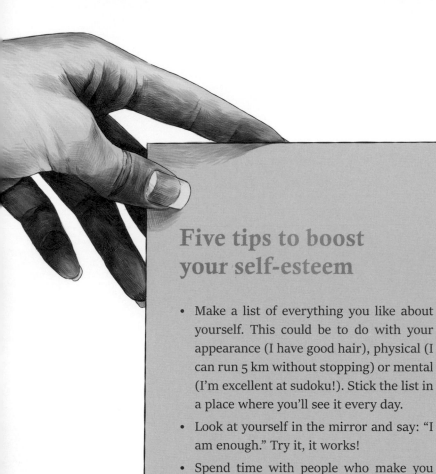

Five tips to boost your self-esteem

- Make a list of everything you like about yourself. This could be to do with your appearance (I have good hair), physical (I can run 5 km without stopping) or mental (I'm excellent at sudoku!). Stick the list in a place where you'll see it every day.

- Look at yourself in the mirror and say: "I am enough." Try it, it works!

- Spend time with people who make you feel good.

- Set yourself a weekly or a monthly personal challenge; perhaps to eat more fruit and veg.

- Learn to accept compliments, rather than rebuff them. Bask in your glory!

THE FIRST TIME WE TAKE THAT FIRST FEARLESS STEP, WE BEGIN TO CHANGE OUR LIVES.

Arianna Huffington

The power of positive thinking

Whole books have been written about the power of positive thinking. This thought technique can increase your sense of self-worth, reduce stress and help you cope better with obstacles that you come up against on the road to greatness. Positive people exude energy, which affects how other people look at them and react to them, which, in turn, opens more doors. Who knows, maybe through one of these may lie a new opportunity, new friends or the path toward your dream job. There's also science to back up the benefits. One research study found that those with a positive frame of mind were one-third less likely to have a heart attack. In another, three different groups of people were shown either happy, neutral or negative images, then given a hypothetical situation. Each group of people was asked how they would react; guess which one dealt with it the best?

133

Your best is

ALWAYS

good enough

Accept your flaws

In the same way that comparing your lifestyle to other people's is unrealistic, so is comparing your body. Who cares if you don't have a perfectly flat stomach, or your knees are a bit knobbly? Your body is your temple, so treat it well. If it's healthy and strong, that's what matters. Learn to love it!

Hanging upside down and being physical makes me feel beautiful.

Pink

Laugh, cry or throw
a tantrum; just do
it with style

No one can make you feel
inferior without your consent.

Eleanor Roosevelt

Confidence boost

Everyone has days when they feel like they can move mountains, and others when they don't even want to lift their head from the pillow. This is normal! All kinds of things can affect how you feel on a given day, from your hormones to the weather. And if you've taken a knock to your confidence – perhaps someone rained on your parade at a recent team meeting – it can be difficult to bounce back. Learn from your mistakes, pick yourself up and dust yourself off. Tomorrow is another day.

Calm your mind

Mindfulness is the practice of quietly noticing what is happening in the present moment. The idea is to try to observe every detail of your surroundings, or of a task you're carrying out, to help you become calmer, less stressed and to achieve a feeling of inner peace and tranquillity. It's quite simple to practise mindfulness yourself and you don't need any special clothing or equipment; there are also lots of videos online about how to become mindful and the benefits it brings. You can even incorporate it into daily tasks such as walking (feel the weight of your feet touching the ground, listen to the crunch of the gravel or your shoes making contact with soft grass) or making a cup of coffee (listen to the sound of the kettle and watch the steam curl through the air in front of you as it boils). Practising mindfulness regularly can also increase your zest for life and boost your self-confidence. Give it a go and relish your rewards.

Grab life by the hand and yell

"let's do this!"

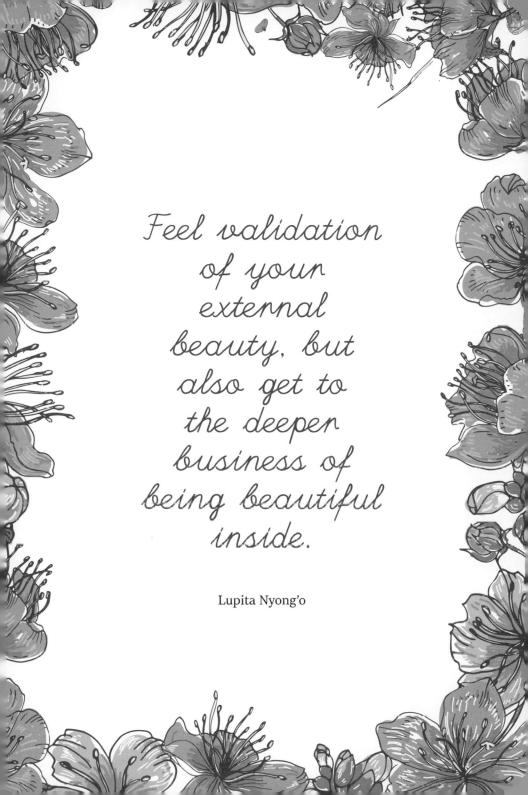

Feel validation of your external beauty, but also get to the deeper business of being beautiful inside.

Lupita Nyong'o

GOOD THINGS MAY COME TO GIRLS WHO WAIT

INCREDIBLE THINGS COME TO GIRLS WHO GO GET 'EM!

Don't dwell

If you've had a bad experience with someone in the past – perhaps someone you thought was a friend turned out not to be the person you thought, or you were treated badly by an ex – you need to let it go. Holding on to negative thoughts and feelings can eat away at you if you let it. If you still have to see the person regularly then rise above, be polite and move on.

DEFINE SUCCESS ON YOUR OWN
TERMS, ACHIEVE IT BY YOUR
OWN RULES, AND BUILD A LIFE
YOU'RE PROUD TO LIVE.

Anne Sweeney

Why do I always think the worst?

We all have those "What if...?" moments. "What if I fail my driving test?" "What if I can't think of anything to say?" "What if nobody at the party likes me?" Unwanted thoughts, or catastrophic thinking, is when we start to imagine things out of all proportion. This kind of thinking can spiral out of control if it's not dealt with, leading to anxiety, stress and more of the same. Worrying about every possible scenario you could encounter won't change the outcome. If you feel like you're slipping into this kind of thinking, stop and take a deep breath. Try practising some of the other tips in this book to improve your mindset. Aim to think rationally and focus on the here and now. Be yourself, do your best; and if the outcome isn't as expected you will be able to deal with it when it happens.

PRINCESSES KEEP THEIR
EYES ON THE PRIZE

Don't sweat the small stuff!

We may think our holiday flight being delayed by an hour is a crisis, but is it really? Many things can seem like the end of the world when they affect our plans, but in the grand scheme of things they probably don't matter. You need only watch the news or take a look online to see that there are bigger problems in the world. Taking a step back and asking yourself whether this will matter in a month, a year, or even five years can put things into perspective **and help** you feel calmer about your situation.

Sideline that stress

Here are a few handy tips to tackle three common stressful situations.

Home emergency: If you can't fix the problem, ask for help or call in an expert. A problem shared is a problem halved.

Standstill traffic: If you're going nowhere, tune the radio to something relaxing and sing along.

A confrontational situation with a friend or colleague: Take a deep breath, count to ten and try not to get angry. If you can, walk away and return when everyone has calmed down.

I HAD TO WORK THE SYSTEM FOR MYSELF, BECAUSE IT WAS NOT GOING TO GIVE ME WHAT I WANTED.

Elizabeth Banks

A healthy body
makes a healthy mind

Keeping your body in tip-top condition has
so many benefits for your brain too. Eating
your five-a-day, drinking in moderation (no
bingeing!) and taking regular exercise are vital
for looking after yourself and can lead to better
quality of sleep and less stress. According to
the World Health Organization, one in four of
us, worldwide, are not active enough – and not
enough physical activity is one of the leading
risk factors of an early demise: now these
sound like good enough reasons to get moving!
You should aim to do at least 150 minutes of
moderate physical activity each week and this
can include anything from household chores,
such as gardening or vacuuming, to walking,
cycling or mountaineering. The choice is
yours! If you have any concerns about your
health or taking up an exercise programme,
always have a chat to your doctor first.

Dreams don't just happen

In today's "instafamous" society, many of us forget that hard work and perseverance are the two most important personal qualities that we need to get us where we want to be. Don't get overwhelmed if something isn't working; keep your chin up and try something different, or look at a problem from a different angle. Good things come to those who work for them.

own it, love it, work it

Conclusion

Hopefully you've found the help and tips in this little guide useful. Not every piece of advice will apply to your specific situation at the moment, but as you travel on down the road of life, the information and inspiration will be here to call upon, should you need it. Women are supportive, loyal and compassionate. We dig deep and summon strength when we have to, we can make the best of a bad situation and, given the right circumstances, we can overcome anything. We learn, we encourage, we are kind; in short, we absolutely rule.

Image credits